10-17-12

Enjoy my book
Dotty

Ephrata Grace E C Church

POEMS by DOTTY

Dotty Kautz

POEMS *by* **DOTTY**

Copyright © 2010
by
Dotty Kautz

All rights reserved.

Library of Congress Number: 2010906304
International Standard Book Number: 978-1-60126-230-1

Printed 2010 by
Masthof Press
219 Mill Road
Morgantown, PA 19543-9516

Welcome to My Book

I was born to Christian parents in Lancaster County, Pennsylvania, and have lived in the County all my life. I had one brother and three sisters—all deceased.

In my late teens I met a young man, and Mel and I were married two years later. God blessed us with five healthy children; one son and four daughters.

Also, twelve grandchildren and nine great-grandchildren have been added to our family with two more expected.

In April of 2003, Mel went Home to our Heavenly Father, after which I started really getting into writing poems.

I hope you are blessed as much in reading my poems as I was in writing them.

God bless you,

Dotty

DEDICATION

I would very much like to dedicate this book to the two men in my life—my deceased husband Mel Kautz, who was the better half of our marriage for almost 54 years until The Lord led him to his Heavenly Home and also my very special friend, Clarence McCoy, who has stood by me through grief, depression and disappointment, but also love and lots of laughter too. I have been really Blessed by The Lord for His bringing these two men into my life.

TABLE OF CONTENTS

A FAREWELL TO MY BEST FRIEND	1
WHAT'S IT LIKE IN HEAVEN?	2
ANOTHER BIRTHDAY CLARENCE	4
I AM ROYALTY	5
WHY DO YOU GO TO CHURCH?	6
THE POTTER AND HIS VESSEL	8
THE LOST SHEEP	9
YOU CAN PRAY	10
THE PRICE OF A RED V.W. CAR	11
MY DREAM	12
MY TALK WITH GOD	13
TOO WARM	14
HOT AND HUMID	14
REDEEMED	15
THE A B C' S OF TRAFFIC	16
TALKING AND LISTENING	17
THE LONG-WINDED PREACHER	18
MY NEW WORLD	20
MY REFLECTION	21
NOAH'S EXPERIENCE	22
BAKING WITH GOD	24
MY LIFE'S BASKET	26
MY FRONT PORCH	27
MY FATHER	28
A NEW BEGINNING	29
WHAT IS A MOTHER	30
MEMORIES	31
FALLING AGAIN IN THE ARMS OF JESUS	32
WATCHING DAD	34
WASTED TIME	35
WHY DO YOU HURT JESUS	36
I SAID A PRAYER	37
I AM SPECIAL	37
A SON GONE BAD	38

ROAD SIGNS	40
SAVED BY THE BOY	42
YOUR LIFE AS AN AUTO	43
GOD'S CAMERA	44
OUR TREASURES	45
MY HANDS	45
THE LITTLE BOAT	46
ARE YOU DIRTY OR CLEAN	48
EMPTY DAYS	49
MARY HAD A LITTLE LAMB	50
BEYOND MY WILDEST DREAMS	51
OUR KITCHEN	52
A MESSAGE TO MY HONEY	53
THANK GOD HE LOVES ME	54
MY PRECIOUS MEMORY	55
LIFE'S JOURNEY	55
LET'S PUT GOD FIRST	56
SAFETY ON BOARD	58
WINTER FUN	59
THE FOUR SEASONS	60
AUTUMN BLESSINGS	61
WILD GEESE	62
MORNING HABITS	63
GOD'S WAY	64
WHAT IS FAITH	65
I AM A BOOK	66
HE'S WATCHING OVER ME	67
MY GOD YOU GAVE ME EVERYTHING	68
ENCOURAGEMENT	69
DOTTY COME HOME	70
A LITTLE ADVICE	71
POST OFFICE JITTERS	72
A SPECIAL OFFERING	74
THE LITTLE OLD COUNTRY CHURCH	76

MY CHINA STORY	78
THE LOST CARROT	79
THE LORD IN MY SHOES	80
A FRIENDLY VISIT	81
MY CAR	82
HAPPY NEW YEAR	83
WHAT IS A VALENTINE	84
PLEASE HELP ME LORD	84
JESUS' RESUME	85
RAGS TO RICHES	85
JESUS' BIRTH AND DEATH	86
MY CHRISTMAS GREETINGS	87
GETTING READY FOR CHRISTMAS	88
THE 4th of JULY	89
MAKING ADJUSTMENTS	90
THANKSGIVING MEMORIES	91
WHAT THANKSGIVING MEANS TO ME	92
SPRING IS HERE	93
HAPPY EASTER	94
MARY AND JOSEPH	95
JESUS' BIRTH	96
A SNOWY SUNDAY MORNING	97

A FAREWELL TO MY BEST FRIEND

It's been three years since you got sick
And it changed our lives forever,
But, no matter how tough everything got
We knew we would always do it together.

I did everything I could
To ease your hurt and pain,
And if I could have had it my way
I'd do it all over again.

But, on Monday morning, God said, "This is enough
Mel, just take me by the hand,
And you and I will take a walk
Right to that promised land."

So he left go of my hand
And grabbed on to a stronger one,
And I could hear God say in a distance
"Well done my son."

Now, don't you worry about me my love
I'm in good hands, you see,
Because, as you and I both know
We raised a wonderful family.

WHAT'S IT LIKE IN HEAVEN?

What's it like in Heaven
Are the streets really paved with gold?
Does it have all that beauty
That we've always been told?

Are there any oceans there
With miles of pure white sand?
Like we had while on vacation
When we would walk, hand in hand?

Do you have family gatherings
When you just sit and talk?
Or, if you have something special to say
Do you take that person for a walk?

How do you celebrate Thanksgiving
Is it done in a special way?
Or, like we should do it down here
And give thanks, every day?

Then, I think about Christmas
And the carols the angels sing,
And, I wonder if you are helping
And does it have that special ring?

Do you have the four seaons there
Spring, summer, winter, fall?
Or, is it only one season
And you enjoy it all?

Now, I was never a stupid person
But, you were always smarter than me,
And I am very curious to find out
How is it there, in Eternity?

(This is a poem I wrote to my husband who went Home to be with our Heavenly Father on April 21, 2003.)

ANOTHER BIRTHDAY CLARENCE

Of all the poems that I've written to you
It always brings me great joy,
BUT, I am running out of words
That rhyme with McCoy.

God has brought you into my life
And YOU are MY very Special Friend,
For I know that you are someone
On whom I can depend.

Now I know when I tell you this
You point your finger towards the sky,
And tell me God's my best friend
BUT, you are too, and I'll tell you why.

I laugh with you and cry with you
And even pray with you too,
And the times we spend together
Are all too few.

So, HAPPY BIRTHDAY (MY FRIEND)
This is another day for you to enjoy,
For God has blessed you for all these years
And you are STILL THE REAL McCOY.

I AM ROYALTY

Many, many years of my life
I was living in spiritual poverty,
And now, because of the grace of God
I became a part of royalty.

Oh, no, I don't wear a crown
Jesus did that for me,
When he took my place on the cross
And was crucified at Calvary.

Now, I'm living on that bountiful food
That only God can prepare,
He alone, knows what's good for me
He has already been there.

I'm so grateful for my new life
That God had planned for me,
And each day I try to thank Him
For bringing me out of poverty.

But, it's been a little hard to believe
That He wanted this sinful me,
To leave all my sinful ways behind
And become part of His royal family.

WHY DO YOU GO TO CHURCH?

Why did you come to church tonight
Didn't you have anything better to do?
Or did you just want to get out of the house
If only, for an hour or two?

Was there nothing good on your T.V.
Or a movie you wanted to view?
Oh, believe me, I know what I'm talking about
I've used some of those excuses too.

Then I came to an old country church
It's one like I've never been in before,
With no paved parking lot, no inside restrooms
But, I did see a welcome mat at the front door.

Now we are a very Special church
And are very casual most every night,
It's a place where we can let our hair down
But, never leaving Jesus out of our sight.

We always have the Reading of the Scriptures
And a powerful time of Prayer,
We are a very needy people
That's another reason why we are there.

One of my favorite parts of the night
Is when everyone joins in and sings the songs,
They are ALL the old hymns
And that is the way it belongs.

We are very BLESSED here at our little church
As we gather each Sunday night,
For we know our SAVIOR is in attendance
Making it so perfectly right.

Now, I ask you again, why are you here tonight
The answer should be very clear,
We want to thank and praise OUR HEAVENLY FATHER
And HONOR HIM WHO WE HOLD DEAR.

THE POTTER AND HIS VESSEL

O LORD, I know You represent many things
But, today, I'll stick to just one,
I'm thinking of You as a potter
And all the hard work You have done.

I know, it took a lot of work
To mold me out of clay,
And I wonder just how much You must do yet
For me to turn out Your way.

I know I still have many rough edges
That You still have to smooth out,
But, as You keep working with me
Your finished vessel will be beautiful, I have no doubt.

So, keep on working with this vessel, LORD
Then, when it's finished and painted too,
I'll be a beautiful vessel, because
I'll BE THERE IN GLORY WITH YOU.

THE LOST SHEEP

There's this little book that I get in the mail
That I use for my devotions each day,
It explains GOD'S Word so clearly
And it's written by His children, by the way.

And I can often relate to it
As the stories do unfold,
But, this one really touched me
About a sheep left out in the cold.

Every evening, just before dark
The farmer would take his sheep into the barn,
And he would always count them
Keeping all free from harm.

But, this one night, one was missing
So he counted and counted again,
He went out to look for his lost sheep
But, that one never made it to the pen.

The next morning, the farmer again looked for that sheep
It was caught on some twine on the ground,
The sheep is alive, the farmer rejoiced, he cried out
THE LOST HAS BEEN FOUND.

Now, as we compare the farmer's lost sheep
To all the human lost sheep who are going astray,
How our Heavenly Father must rejoice
When just ONE comes HIS way.

Now, I said that this illustration touched me
It's because I once was a farmer too,
And I'm also rejoicing that our Heavenly Father
Wants to take care of ME and YOU.

YOU CAN PRAY

As I sit here at my desk
Deeply involved with my devotions,
The wind is blowing so briskly outside
Giving me mixed emotions.

Now, I never cared for all that wind
It always seemed so scary to me,
But, I have a friend who really loves it
And the windier, the happier she would be.

Now, isn't it nice that we're all different
GOD made us just that way,
For if we were all alike
Some of us wouldn't be needed today.

But, we are all very needy people
And need GOD'S tender care,
And we always get much closer to HIM
When we talk to HIM in prayer.

Now, GOD needs each one of us
To do HIS work today,
And, if you think you can't do anything
THINK AGAIN, YOU CAN PRAY.

THE PRICE OF A RED V.W. CAR

I heard of this lady who went to a Safari
She was driving her red V.W. car,
And, soon after the tour had started
She realized she wouldn't get very far.

There was an elephant in the driving lane
And she couldn't go around,
She laid on the horn for him to move
But, he didn't like that sound.

He squatted down on the hood of her car
With damages, you wouldn't believe,
The manager came to help her
And good advice, she did receive.

The manager said that the elephants are trained
That when a horn blows, they sit on a red ball,
Now, how was that elephant supposed to know
That her red V.W. wasn't a red ball, at all?

Soon after the lady left, she came upon an accident
She went around and didn't stop,
She looked in her mirror and saw something flashing
Oh yes, it was the COP.

He said, "You just can't leave an accident like that"
Thinking that she was involved too,
But, after telling him what really happened
He wondered if that was false, or, could it be true?

She went to the car dealership when the Cop was finished
And told them what she had done,
They took one look at her Broken-down V.W.
And gave her a Brand New One.

They put her red V.W. up on their Business roof
With a sign that had this little pun,
WE SELL VERY DEPENDABLE CARS HERE
AN ELEPHANT SAT ON ME AND I STILL RUN!

MY DREAM

When I got awake this morning
I was having a dream,
I was puzzled, so I asked The Lord
Just what does this mean?

He said, "Dotty, do you know you own a Bed and Breakfast
And you are doing your very best?
As you smile and shake the hand
Of each and every guest.

You try to make them comfortable
So they enjoy their stay,
And hope that they will come back
Again, some other day.

I know you are enjoying
Every person who you touch,
And you go about your business
And hope that they enjoy it, just as much.

Now, I'm watching you Dotty
So keep doing your very best,
For you just never know
When I'LL BE YOUR NEXT GUEST."

I think that there is a message here
That GOD is trying to say,
"Prepare yourself, work hard for ME
For I'm coming back one day.

And I want you to be ready
For the time is getting short,
AND NEVER, NEVER FORGET
The ball is ALWAYS IN MY COURT."

MY TALK WITH GOD

I had a Special conversation
With GOD just the other day,
And what HE said, stunned me
And I didn't know what to say.

He said, "I love talking with all of you down there
But, you must understand,
We have to talk more often
Not just when you need a helping hand."

He said, "Most people get up each morning
And go on their merry way,
Then, when trouble comes their way
They want to look, MY WAY."

I said, "GOD, you are always right
We are the ones to be blamed,
And as I look here at myself
I feel so ashamed."

So GOD, please forgive me
When I do that to you,
He said, "I FORGIVE YOU MY CHILD
I ALWAYS DO."

TOO WARM

It's been too warm for this winter
Warmer than I can ever remember,
It really doesn't feel like January
But, more like September.

I just don't understand this weather
But, it must be of GOD'S will,
For He surely is helping us out
With our HEATING BILL.

So, enjoy this weather while you can
For you just never know,
When you will look out your window
And see what we call snow.

HOT AND HUMID

It's been so humid these last few days
With just no breeze at all,
But, it won't last that much longer
As we will be entering into fall.

The kids will be going back to college
And the younger ones to school,
And the weather will turn to, yes, you guessed it
C—O—O—L.

So, thank you Lord for another summer
Another summer for me to serve,
And thanks for ALL YOUR BLESSINGS
THAT I JUST DON'T DESERVE.

REDEEMED

I listened to a preacher
On tape, just today,
And he gave me the inspiration
For this poem I'm sending your way.

He talked about redemption
And how we must press on,
And serve our Precious Savior
Before our life is gone.

He compared us to those green stamps
That we saved many years ago,
Then we could get lots of great things
Without spending very much dough.

But, he said that as long as those green stamps
Were only pressed on a page,
They were very worthless
But, got more valuable with age.

You remember, we had to go
Directly to a Green Stamp Store,
And when we redeemed them
They were worth so much more.

Well, I've been redeemed
And when God calls me at whatever age,
I'm ready to meet my Savior because
I'm more than a green stamp on a page.

THE A B C' S OF TRAFFIC

A—Always be very careful
B—Before you cross the street
C—Caution is a good word
D—Don't look down at your feet.

E—Every step is easy
F—First you look ahead,
G—Go when the light is green
H—Hold when it is red.

I—If you are talking to a friend
J—Just keep this in mind,
K—Keep your eyes on the traffic
L—Lots of them are not very kind.

M—Make your traveling easy
N—No one will object,
O—Open your sense of direction
P—Perhaps no one will suspect.

Q—Quickly the light will turn yellow, so
R—Really get ready to stop,
S—So you will be prepared
T—To not trip or take a flop.

U—Usually when you are driving YOUR CAR
V—Various laws are very hard,
W—Will you be alert to see that
X—X, means, there's a CROSSING GUARD???

Y—You know God is riding with you
      You are never alone,
Z—Z means be cautious
      You are in a SCHOOL ZONE.

TALKING AND LISTENING

Have you talked to God today
If not, why not?
Was it that you were too busy
Or that you just forgot?

Oh, He is that One Special Friend
Who cares the most for you,
And as He sits there on His throne
He watches everything you do.

Is He pleased with what He sees
As He looks down here on you?
Or are there things in your life
That you could change from old to new?

I'm so glad that I have this Special Father
That I can talk to every day,
And to know He's always listening
And showing me how to do things, His way.

THE LONG-WINDED PREACHER

There was this long-winded preacher
Who got so wrapped up in God's Word,
He preached so long to his congregation
They forgot all that they had heard.

The congregation got so bored
They got up and walked out one by one,
The preacher called after them saying
"Hey, I'm still not done."

Well, his wife was so embarrassed
And knew there was something they had to do,
To keep the parishioners happy
And cemented to their pew.

So she gave him a life-saver to put in his pocket
Then when he started to preach,
He put the life-saver in his mouth
And everything else out of reach.

When the life-saver was all gone
Because, the life-saver was his prop,
He knew it was time to wrap things up
And that he had to stop.

Well, this was great for a couple of weeks
Everything went so well,
And everyone in the congregation was happy
And loved the preacher, you could tell.

Then, one Sunday, it happened again
He preached on and on and on,
He thought he had plenty of time
Because, His life-saver still wasn't gone.

Again, people walked out, one by one
The preacher got so depressed,
He apologized to them all
But, also knew, he had done his best.

He took the life-saver out of his mouth
And his face got really, really red,
For he hadn't put a life-saver in
But, it was a coat button, instead.

MY NEW WORLD

My children introduced me to this electronic world
And it's all new to me,
They got me this tiny little cell phone
They say, it's for my security.

I told them, I will not answer it
While I am out there driving,
Because I think more of my life
And I'd rather be surviving.

Now, you'd think this would be enough
For me to learn to do,
But, no, just last week there came
One of those computers too.

Now, this computer is like a new toy
And my time on it should be restricted,
So please Lord, will you help me
I don't want to become addicted?

MY REFLECTION

When I look into my mirror
Do you know what I see?
I see that God had a sense of humor
When He created me.

He could have given me just one big eye
And left off the mouth and nose,
Also, the hair and ears
Could have been omitted, I suppose.

I'm glad that He knew what He was doing
When He put all those parts inside my body,
And I wonder too, if He suspected
That my parents would call me, Dotty.

He gave me a great big heart
So I could share with others,
And He showed me how to love
My sisters and my brothers.

So, thank you Lord, for my life
And I might be a little bold,
But, after You created me
I sure hope you threw away the mold.

NOAH'S EXPERIENCE

I wonder just how it was
I guess it could have been dark,
When God spoke to Noah and said
"I want you to build an ark."

And I want it to be a big one
A very big one, you see,
Because it must carry a lot of passengers
For all of them to be set free.

God told Noah to get his wife
And all his family too,
And put them on this ark that you build
And I'll take care of you.

I'm going to send down a lot of rain
And it could last for forty days,
And I want you to help me
And do it in many ways.

I want you to count the animals
As they get on the ark for you,
There will be two of each species
Oh yes, two of each will do.

Then as it continues to rain
And until the ark can sail away,
Noah, get a good night's sleep
For tomorrow is another big day.

When all are aboard and the water is deep enough
For the ark to set sail,
I'll be with you all the way
There's no reason for my plan to fail.

Now, the ark took off on its special voyage
Just as God did command,
When they saw the dove with the olive leaf
They knew they would soon see dry land.

Now, Noah must have had a lot of faith in God
To do what God told him to do,
And I pray that my ears will let me hear
When God speaks to me too.

BAKING WITH GOD

When you decide
You want to bake a cake,
The first decision is
What kind will you make.

Then you check out your cupboard
To make sure it isn't bare,
And you hope that all the ingredients you need
Are really, really there.

You pull out your mixer
And make sure the bowl is clean,
And the same with your utensils
If you know what I mean.

The ingredients that you combine
Are usually eggs, butter, sugar and flour,
You pop it in the oven at 350
And it's done in about half an hour.

When it is done and you let it cool
The icing goes on top,
And you can be very satisfied
If your finished product doesn't flop.

Now, some ingredients in my life are
Peace, compassion, understanding, and love,
But, I wouldn't have any of this
If it wasn't for God above.

When right ingredients put together
Turns into a beautiful cake,
And ingredients God has given us
A wonderful person it can make.

So, check out what your ingredients are
Because wonders never cease,
And follow God's recipe completely
He wants us for His masterpiece.

MY LIFE'S BASKET

As fall is just around the corner
And the days are getting cool,
I think about my life's basket
And whether it's empty or full.

I know God wants me to be happy
With no bitterness, gossip, envy, or pride,
And also self ambition, worry, and lust
Are all sins that form inside.

I wonder when you read your Bible
And you feel it's not speaking to you,
And God seems to be at a distance
And you have a different point of view.

Then, when you go to church
And you just sit there and stare,
And you get nothing out of the worship service
It's like, you weren't even there.

Then you go home and start a new week
And everything's the same,
Nothing seems to go right
And you find places to put the blame.

Well, God is trying to get your attention
And whether we listen or not,
He is the one who is in control
And, He loves us all, a lot.

So please God, take all these sins from my life
Even if you have to yank and pull,
For when I stand before you on judgment day
I need a basket that is full.

MY FRONT PORCH

As I sit here on my front porch
Trying to enjoy God's creation,
Some of the creatures He created
Are having a celebration.

The rabbits are hopping across the lawn
Without a worry or a care,
They are having so much fun
It's like, I'm not even there.

The squirrels run across my banister
And all my plants they have destroyed,
I worked so hard to plant them
So now, I really am annoyed.

Every morning when I get up
And look out my front door,
I know the squirrels were partying again
They left their nuts all over the floor.

The birds were enjoying the party too
They didn't have to fly very far,
And the reason I know this for sure
They left their deposits all over my car.

I thoroughly enjoy my front porch
I talk to my neighbors as they walk by,
And while lying on my lounge chair
Sometimes I even get a little shut-eye.

But, I do love my front porch
It gives me time to think things through,
So, I guess I must share it with my furry friends
GOD HAS MADE THEM TOO.

MY FATHER

What do I remember about My Father
Well, He was short and had a beard,
And although He wasn't a big man
He was someone who I feared.

I came along later in His life
He was forty-six when I arrived,
And although I wasn't planned for
I'm sure He was happy that I survived.

He never said that He loved me
But, they didn't do that in those days,
He showed me that He cared for me
In many other ways.

I never called Him Father
I always called Him DAD,
But He always had a punishment for me
When He thought that I was bad.

He wanted me to marry a farmer
But that was not the life for me,
He didn't want me to marry Mel
But a farmer's wife, I didn't want to be.

He did finally get to like Mel
He saw just how much Mel loved me,
And I think that He was proud
Of Mel and MY FAMILY.

Now if you are listening to me Dad
I know you're there with God,
And I think I turned out to be a SPECIAL PERSON
BECAUSE, YOU DIDN'T SPARE THE ROD.

A NEW BEGINNING

It was one fine day in July
In nineteen ninety-eight,
I was asked to sing at a local church
And a member there said, "Now don't be late."

So I arrived a little bit early
And as I entered the front door,
I saw all those strange faces
Wearing smiles and smiles galore.

We sang two songs I remember
And our voices really soared,
For we were so excited
To make a joyful noise unto The Lord.

The pastor preached a great sermon
And as I was leaving my pew,
So many folks shook my hand and said
"It was good to see you."

Now, all those people seemed sincere
And right there out of the blue,
I had gotten acquainted
With Christian friends, I never knew.

As I walked out that front door
I was smiling from cheek to cheek,
'Cause I knew right then and there
I'd be back again, NEXT WEEK.

I hadn't gone to any church
For about ten years, you see,
And the miracle of this story is
Now, my husband goes with me.

WHAT IS A MOTHER

A MOTHER is someone who loves her husband
And makes a happy home,
She keeps her FAMILY safely
Under the FAMILY DOME.

She loves her children very much
For them there's nothing she wouldn't do,
She feeds them, clothes them, loves them
And even prays for them too.

A MOTHER is someone SPECIAL
Who her CHILDREN can look up to,
And when her CHILDREN are all grown up
She is proud of what they do.

Now, this is what I remember about MY MOTHER
She was a dedicated CHRISTIAN, you see,
So THANKS for being such a WONDERFUL MOM
And for leaving your great LEGACY to me.

M—is for the MANY times she prayed for me
O—is for ONLY that she cared for me so much,
T—is for all those TEARS she cried
H—is for those HANDS with her gentle touch,
E—is for EVERY TIME we spoke on the phone
R—is for the RIGHTEOUS person she was

NOW THIS WAS MY PRECIOUS MOTHER
AND SHE LOVED ME—JUST BECAUSE.

MEMORIES

Today, I went back to the church
The one we attended when I was being raised,
And they have made so many changes
That I was so amazed.

In fact, the original building is no longer standing
They just built around it,
And as I sat there reminiscing
Nothing seemed familiar about it.

You see, I was raised by Christian parents
We went to Sunday school and church every week,
When I was old enough to have Jesus in my life
I was baptized out in a creek.

It was also the church where I walked down the aisle
And said those two big words, "I Do,"
We raised our five children there
And each one became Christians too.

I did a lot of thinking there today
Looking back on how things used to be,
But, time has a way of marching on
And that's O.K. with me.

Now I'm wondering if things will change as much
In the next sixty years as it has in the past,
But, I know God has everything under control
And I don't worry because

I'LL BE IN MY HEAVENLY HOME AT LAST!

FALLING AGAIN IN THE ARMS OF JESUS

One Sunday night My Friend was leaving my home
And I wanted to close my front door,
The sole of my shoe caught on my carpet
And you guessed it, I fell to the floor.

Oh, I laid there for a while
As I realized just what I had done,
Then I examined all my bones
To make sure I hadn't broken one.

Well, everything seemed to be O.K.
I didn't even shed a tear,
But, my next problem was
How in the world do I get up from here?

My purse was lying on the floor
And in it was my cell phone,
I thought I can call someone
I don't have to lay here all alone

But, I didn't want to tell my kids
That I was lying here all alone,
Because they are looking for any excuse
To put me in a Nursing Home.

No, that's not true about the Nursing Home
They don't want me to go there at all,
So, they will just have to take care of me
Each and every time I fall.

I crawled over to the sofa
And getting up was quite an ordeal,
Because, ever since my knee replacement
I can no longer kneel.

I walked back to my bedroom
And thought, gee, I'm O.K.
Now, if you don't mind Dotty
Let's just keep it that way.

As I sat on my bed, I was reminded
Of the poem I had read at church that very night,
About GOD always watching over me
Never once leaving me out of His sight.

So, thank you Lord for another blessing
You always do everything right,
And, I felt it was your hand pulling me up
From my floor, that Sunday night.

WATCHING DAD

I heard this country western song
Just the other day,
That inspired me to write this poem
So I'm sending it your way.

It had nothing to do with trucks or gambling
Or drinking, NO, none of the above,
It was simply about a man and his child
And a whole lot of LOVE.

You see, as this young boy was playing
He used a four-letter word,
The father was so stunned
At what he had just heard.

In amazement, the father asked his son
"Where did you hear that word that was so bad?"
The boy looked up and replied,
"I'VE BEEN WATCHING YOU, DAD."

That night the father went into his son's room
To tuck him into bed,
He saw his son on his knees
His hands folded and a bowed head.

He listened, as his son prayed
And thanked God for a good day,
Father was so amazed and asked him,
"How did you learn to pray that way?"

He answered, "I have a GREAT TEACHER
And I'm really not that bad,
Because you see, I've learned a lot
I'VE BEEN WATCHING YOU, DAD!"

WASTED TIME

I can't believe, it's almost September
The time goes by so fast,
And as I look on my life of this past year
I wonder, what I've done for Christ that will last.

I wonder, is He pleased with me in all that I do
Or, have I rejected Him in some way?
I know He puts obstacles in my path
But, He helps me through them every day.

When I think things are really going well
And everything seems O.K.,
Here comes another situation
That GOD sends my way.

He's been doing that quite a bit lately
I think my attention, He's trying to get,
Or, maybe, He's just testing me
To see if I'll get upset.

I wonder, does GOD test our patience
When He knows there's something we need?
And also, knowing how frail we are
Without Him, we would never succeed.

I'm so glad I have this Heavenly Father
Watching me at every turn,
But, even in my golden years
I know there's still so much to learn.

So, take my hand LORD and never let go
With you, I'll never go the wrong way,
And as we walk together, LORD
I KNOW EVERYTHING WILL BE O.K.

WHY DO YOU HURT JESUS

Why do you hurt JESUS the way that you do
He gave HIS life for me and for you,
HE looks down from HEAVEN with great agony
As HE watches your actions, just what does HE see?

Your BIBLE just lying there, collecting dust
For you never read it unless it's a must,
And you spend so little time in prayer
Do you think you don't need it, or just don't you care?

Yes, you attend church quite regularly
And you enjoy the fellowship, it's plain to see,
But, as the offering plate comes by your pew
If it wasn't for envelopes, just what would you do?

WHY do you hurt JESUS the way that you do
Isn't it enough that HE died for you?
Now, if you decide that you really don't care
THINK, when you get to Heaven's Gate
WILL JESUS CARE?

I SAID A PRAYER

I said a Special Prayer for you again today
I asked GOD to watch over you and make sure that you're O.K.,
I asked Him to cradle you in His arms, to hold you that Special way
Then with His strong, yet gentle hands, brush all your hurt away.

I asked Him to give you peace of mind in everything you do
And to remind you daily, how much He does love you,
So keep your faith and trust in Him, that's all that you can do
Then please believe me when I say, "This friend is praying for you."

I AM SPECIAL

I am someone Special, GOD made me just this way,
He gave me different talents, that I can use each day.

He walks with me and talks to me, He tells me that I am His own,
He carries me over the thistles of life, He knows I can't do it alone.

I come in contact with people each day, some of them I never knew,
But, GOD brings us together, because they are Special too.

A SON GONE BAD

There was a man who had two sons
And one day when the father was alone,
The youngest son requested his inheritance
He wanted to go out on his own.

So the father forked over the money
And his son walked down the road,
Little did the young son realize
He soon would be carrying a heavy load.

He enjoyed his new life with all its wealth
And living a life of sin,
All the women were so contented
Just to be, [with him].

Well, the time came when the money was all gone
And he began to wonder, why?
All the women had turned against him
They had all said, [Bye-Bye].

So, with the money gone and no friends to be with
He no longer felt very big,
And having to eat, he got a job
Feeding pig, after pig, after pig.

He got to feeling just how good he had it
At home, at his father's table,
He could go home and ask his father
To be his servant, if he was able.

Now, I don't know what all that he had done
Or even how long it had been
But, the father saw him coming
And welcomed him home again.

But, big brother was jealous and very annoyed
And he started to attack,
For the young son was given rings and a robe
And he didn't want his brother back.

Big brother thought his father was unfair
And could think of him, at least,
But, father only thought of his youngest son
And decided to have a feast.

I think the moral of this story is
When we choose to live a life of sin,
Jesus is so thrilled to forgive and welcome us
Back into his loving arms, again.

ROAD SIGNS

As we go on our journey here on earth
There are many choices we can make,
And we must be very careful
Just which path we take.

Sometimes, we get to a [Y] in the road
And we don't know which way to turn,
But, if Jesus is right there beside us
He will help us learn.

Now, with all the choices that we have
In our busy life today,
It does not take much energy
For the Devil to lead us astray.

Then when we are slipping away from God
And the Devil thinks he is on top,
Jesus puts a sign in front of us
A big sign that says, [STOP].

When He allows us to continue on our way
He wants our old bridges for us to burn,
Then we can see another sign
Oh, yes, it is a [U] turn.

Now, if we choose to follow that [U] turn
We will be headed the other way,
And Jesus and His followers will rejoice
Oh, what a glorious day.

Now, we're told that the road to Heaven is narrow
And not everyone will find it,
This sounds a little scary
So, we must be reminded.

There's also this sign that says [NO PARKING],
And I think that's God's way of telling me
To get off my easy-chair and talk to the unsaved
How, Jesus can and will set them free.

So, as we travel this highway of life
Please stay between the lines,
And allow Jesus to take the steering wheel
He knows about all those road signs.

SAVED BY THE BOY

There was this young boy
Who was walking on the beach,
And as he looked out over the water
He knew those waves were way out of his reach.

So he picked up a starfish
Lying at the water's edge on the sand,
Feeling a little bit sad for it
As he held it in his hand.

He threw it back into the water
Not knowing if it was still alive,
But, with a big smile on his face
He hoped it would survive.

He got down on his knees and said,
"Jesus, I don't want this starfish to die,"
And as he got up, he saw
A stranger walking by.

The man asked the boy what he was doing
He said that he was saving fish,
The man laughed as he looked down the long beach
He said, "You can't save all those fish."

The boy, looking up at the smug man's face
Feeling very proud for what he had just done,
Said, "Yes, I know mister,
But, I did save that one."

YOUR LIFE AS AN AUTO

Is your life like that of an automobile
Running smoothly, when everything's fine?
Your engine's a purring, your tires have good tread
And your body has such a great shine?

Then, along comes a bump in the road and you will find
Your car will come close to a halt,
So what do you do, do you just give up
And say, it's the other guy's fault?

Now, the life of a Christian is so very hard
You get bumped and scratched so much,
But, just like a car, you can remedy that
With a hammer, then the touch of a brush.

So, pound out your dents and have an oil change
Then, fill up your tank with Hi-Test,
And if you keep going you surely will find
That the Lord will take care of the rest.

GOD'S CAMERA

This little girl had to walk
To her elementary school every day,
But, this day was different because
A bad storm was headed their way.

The mother was quite concerned
As afternoon classes were leaving out,
For the storm was getting stronger
With lightning flashing all about

So she drove towards the school
To give her child a ride home,
And as she saw her daughter approaching
Mother knew she wasn't alone.

For every time there was a flash of lightning
The child would smile and look up to the sky,
And mother was so puzzled
So she asked her daughter, why?

Her reply was, "I want to look pretty
Because God is taking a picture of me."
And even there as a child she knew
God was keeping her company.

Now, I have always hated thunderstorms
And never thought of God as taking a picture of me,
But, this young brave child gave me a reminder
That no matter what, God is taking care of me.

OUR TREASURES

Last week we were hit with a national disaster
And it destroyed some of our southern states,
And I wondered Lord, how many were ready
To meet you at those pearly gates.

The Bible says, "Don't store up treasures on earth
Where moth and rust doth corrupt today,
But, store up for yourself treasures in Heaven
And please do it without delay."

God wants us to praise and glorify Him
And keep away from all worldly pleasures,
So, as we continue our daily walk
Where are we storing our treasures?

MY HANDS

Oh Lord, as I look here at my hands
Just what will I do with them today?
Will I use them just for my own good
And in my own selfish way?

Or, should I use them to call a friend
And make sure that they are O.K.?
Or Lord, do you have something else
You wish for me to do today?

If you wish, I could write another poem
I know you make no demands,
But, please Lord, keep a watchful eye
On these aging hands.

THE LITTLE BOAT

I heard a story recently
About this special boy,
He was interested in boats
And this he did enjoy.

So one day, he got some wood
And built his very own boat,
He tied a string to it, put it in a stream
Just to see if it would float.

Well, that little boat did take off
And down the stream it went,
The boy held on to the other end of the string
Not knowing the boat's intent.

The boy followed the boat down the stream
Until the attached string tore,
He watched the little boat sail away
Until he could see it no more.

I believe this boy was very sad
For it caught him by surprise,
And as he walked back to his house
He wiped away the tears from his eyes.

Sometime later, he went into a local pawn shop
Just to look around,
And as he walked back this one aisle
You won't believe what he found.

Yes, it was his precious little boat
He picked it up and held it tight,
He paid the merchant his asking price
But, never once left it out of his sight.

He said, "I made you, now I bought you
You are my very own,
You are so special to me
And I'll never leave you alone."

This is what Jesus did for all of us
He made us, then He bought us too,
And as He hung there on that cross
His love for us came shining through.

ARE YOU DIRTY OR CLEAN

As I got up this morning
My face was all aglow,
As I went to the window
And look out and saw the snow.

It was such a pretty sight to see
So white and fresh and clean,
For it had covered up all that dirt
Not even one speck could be seen.

It stayed that way for awhile
'Til cars drove back the street,
And the paperboy made tracks
With his tiny little feet.

That's how it is with our lives
When we allow Satan to take the lead,
He makes us so very dirty
And doesn't even fulfill our need.

Then, we must talk to Jesus
And every Sin confess,
And He will wash us white like snow
With His own tenderness.

But, then we must be on our guard
For we don't know exactly when,
That old Satan will sneak around
To make us dirty again.

EMPTY DAYS

Do you have days when you are sad
And you feel you're all alone?
You know, you can always talk to Jesus
On His Royal Telephone.

Yes, you will get quite a tingling
There are NO BUSY SIGNALS THERE,
And He can TALK away your worries
And relieve you of every care.

You will also get excited
For you are never put ON HOLD,
And the time you spend together
Is more precious then pure gold.

So go ahead, use this SPECIAL LINE
Just put it to the test,
Then when you look back on this day
You can say, "IT WAS THE BEST."

MARY HAD A LITTLE LAMB

We all remember Mary who had a little lamb
His fleece was pure white like snow,
And always when Mary would go away
That Lamb would also go.

One day when Mary went to school
The lamb wasn't far behind,
The children left the lamb in their room
And the teacher didn't mind.

Soon the rules got more strict
But, the children were not to blame,
The Lamb of God was banned from school
And this was quite a shame.

As time went by, things got so much worse
As month after month turned into years,
With God left out of the classroom
There came gun shots and tears.

We have to stop this terrible crime
That our children are facing today,
So, allow that Lamb in school again
And teach our children how to pray.

BEYOND MY WILDEST DREAMS

When I go to bed at night
I'm tired, or so it seems,
And as I lay there, drifting off to sleep
I anticipate, maybe some dreams.

It could be a funny one
Or, even a little scary,
It could even make your hair stand up
But, it would be nice if it were merry.

Sometimes, I wonder just how it will be
The day I take my last breath,
Will my loved ones be waiting for me
Where there's no more sickness, or death?

Will Jesus be reaching out for me
As He stands at that pearly gate?
If so, I know He will be on time
Because, He is never late.

And what is the first thing that I will see
When I reach that Promised Land?
Could it be that glorious mansion
That God so generously planned?

I often think about Heaven
Where there's no insurance or bills to pay,
And no moving from house to house
God has picked out where I shall stay.

Will I know my husband, my mom and dad
My brother and sisters too?
And all my precious offspring that are left
When God says, "Dotty, I'm coming for you."

Oh, my, a lot is going to take place
And I can't fathom all that it means,
But, one thing I can safely say
It's beyond my wildest dreams.

OUR KITCHEN

Do you remember our last kitchen
It was quaint, but, a little small?
We had a lot of good meals in there
And played games too as I recall.

Many times when I was working in there
You would give me a love-pat on my rear,
And I can distinctly remember saying
"Not now, Dear."

In these last seven years since you've been gone
I would often see you standing at the sink,
And it wasn't to wash the dishes
You just needed a drink.

A magnet on our fridge said, "Stay out of my kitchen"
And you realized it was only a plaque,
But, oh what I wouldn't give
Just to have you back.

But, I know you're at a much better place
With our Heavenly Father and the angels, too,
And only He knows the exact time
When He will unite me again with you.

A MESSAGE TO MY HONEY

Today, it is but one year
Since you left for your Heavenly Home,
I love you and I miss you
But, you left me here all alone.

I know the angels are rejoicing
And God is happy too,
That you were one of His children
And He cared so much for you.

Now, you keep watching over me
And with God's help, I will get by,
And I promise you that one day
I'll meet you at our Mansion in the sky.

THANK GOD HE LOVES ME

When I was just a little girl
Approximately three,
I went to Sunday School every week
'Cause teacher said, "JESUS LOVES ME."

Then I grew to be a teenager
I was so happy and carefree,
Of course, I had Christian parents
THANK GOD THEY LOVED ME.

It was just a few years later
That I met my husband-to-be,
And I whisper a prayer every night
THANK GOD HE LOVES ME.

I was fortunate to have children
Four girls and a boy, you see,
They each in their own way try to please me
THANK GOD THEY LOVE ME.

I got mixed up with a bad crowd
I smoked, I drank, I swore,
And I just couldn't see how
GOD COULD LOVE ME ANYMORE.

One night while lying in bed
A voice called, "Come to me,"
I answered, "LORD, HERE I AM"
THANK GOD, HE SAVED ME.

MY JESUS died upon the CROSS
From MY SINS, HE SET ME FREE,
And that's why I'm so very happy
BECAUSE MY JESUS STILL LOVES ME.

MY PRECIOUS MEMORY

I have lots of photo albums
That mean so much to me,
For in each photograph
Is a SPECIAL MEMORY.

When GOD took my husband HOME
I thought it just couldn't be,
But now I understand because
He left me a PRECIOUS MEMORY.

And as I look up to the sky
For as far as I can see,
I thank my Heavenly Father
For my PRECIOUS MEMORY.

LIFE'S JOURNEY

As we travel on life's journey
On these fast highways here below,
We have so many things to do
And so many places we must go.

That we seem to neglect our Heavenly Father
And how we are to serve,
He supplies us with everything
And this we don't deserve.

We know that the road to Heaven is narrow
And few there be that find it,
This sounds like a scary thing
So we must be reminded.

Now, watch out for those big highways
And try to concentrate,
And keep looking for that narrow path
That leads to HEAVEN'S GATE.

LET'S PUT GOD FIRST

I go to this little country church
Almost every Sunday night,
Each one cares about the other one
And going there is such a delight.

One night the leader asked
If someone would like to tell how they've been blessed,
One lady stood up
And this subject, she addressed.

She said that she couldn't sleep at night
And tried taking different kinds of pills,
But no matter what she took
It didn't help to cure her ills.

One day when she was driving to work
In her chest she got some pain,
She just kept right on driving
Hoping it would leave again.

Well it didn't, it just got worse
And she wondered if she should wait,
For to see a doctor or go to the hospital
Not wanting to wait until it was too late.

She did go to the hospital
And had the tests done that they always do,
A cardiogram, an E.K.G.
Just to name few.

Then she realized she had taken some pills
That might not have agreed with her,
And as she talked to her doctor about it
On this they did concur.

That's when Our Heavenly Father took over
He was there all the time,
Wondering why she didn't come to Him first
Then everything would have been fine.

I think we all learned a good lesson that night
As she stood there telling her interesting story,
And I think God put her through all those channels
So she could give HIM—ALL THE GLORY.

SAFETY ON BOARD

I read a story the other day
About two boats out at sea,
That gave me the idea for this poem
So, here it comes from me.

On the one boat, sitting on the Captain's Chair
Was JESUS CHRIST, OUR LORD,
And the boat was navigated calmly
And everyone felt safe on board.

The Mother and Father sat peacefully
And the Children played joyfully around them,
And that helped them to understand
How much GOD loved all of them.

Now, with the second boat, it was much the same
But, with those parents, there was much despair,
For the Father wanted CHRIST on the boat
BUT, NOT ON THE CAPTAIN'S CHAIR.

As the Father steered the boat
The Mother was desperately trying,
For the Children were all wet and cold
And sadly crying.

Is it like that with us today
We want to take the lead,
And when it is comfortable for us
We can always pick up speed.

Now, please take care of YOURSELF
You know, GOD really does care,
And be perfectly sure YOU ALWAYS know
WHO'S SITTING ON YOUR CAPTAIN'S CHAIR.

WINTER FUN

We were having a very mild winter
At least it started out that way,
Then that GROUNDHOG SAW HIS SHADOW
Now we have six more weeks to pay.

Well we finally did get some snow
But with it came sleet and rain,
And along with all that shoveling
Came a few aches and pains.

All week long, people were shoveling to get out
Some stayed in for a good long while,
I was in that second class of people
Digging at all that ice is not my style.

Now I hear we're to get more snow
With ice, like we did last week,
And the shoveling will start all over again
In fact, it will all be a repeat.

But, I know GOD knows what He is doing
And a mistake, HE will never make,
And I am so happy that HE knows
Which path that snow and sleet will take.

So let's just try to accept it
And each time we walk out the door,
THINK OF THAT OLD GROUNDHOG
IT'S ONLY FOR A FEW WEEKS MORE!!

THE FOUR SEASONS

You know we have four seasons, spring, summer, winter, fall,
But, do we really take the time to appreciate them all?

Yes, winter is a beautiful time when those snowflakes cover the ground,
When you stand inside your window, everything is white all around.

Then, after a few months, spring is here and everything comes alive,
With all the spring flowers popping up, a harsh winter they did survive.

Ah yes, then here comes summer, when we can shed some clothes,
And enjoy the fruits of our labor and go on vacation, I suppose.

Then it's time for the fall and it gets a little cool,
All the crops are harvested and the kids go back to school.

Now we've completed all the seasons and we start another year,
But, did we really enjoy each one at the time when it was here?

You might be wondering why I write this, so I'll do my best,
Because it's my way of getting things off my chest.

I went into a store today and remember, it's still September,
A lady there was buying things she will use to decorate in December.

And I just thought, I want to enjoy all the things that we have, NOW,
The beautiful leaves, the falling of the leaves,
    the raking of the leaves, Somehow.

God gave us ALL these seasons, if we don't take advantage of them, I fear,
That we will lose all He has for us,
    because, we've LOST ANOTHER YEAR.

AUTUMN BLESSINGS

As I look out my window
And see all those leaves coming down,
I know GOD is telling me something
Another season is coming around.

I love all those beautiful colors
As they still hang there on the tree,
GOD has painted that beautiful picture
And HE did it for you and for me.

And with all those leaves a'falling
I know a lot of work it will take,
But, I'll rely on my hefty leaf bag
And my faithful rake.

I'll think of each leaf as a BLESSING
And watch as they surmount,
And think of all the BLESSINGS GOD gives me
Many more than I could ever count.

Now, as I anticipate this Autumn Job
It will be another BLESSING for me,
When I can look up and make sure that
THERE'S NO MORE LEAVES ON THAT TREE.

WILD GEESE

It was just this week, I heard
That old familiar sound in the sky,
And as I looked up I could see
All those wild geese flying by.

I just stood there and watched them
It was so interesting to see,
As they floated in that formation
In the shape of that special [V].

They seemed to be so contented
And I could hear their joyful coo,
I thought how great it was
They had a faithful leader too.

That made me think of God
And how He leads us every day,
And if we are faithful to Him
He will take us all the way.

To that Mansion He is preparing for us
And just like the wild geese flew,
I am traveling toward my new home
What about you?

MORNING HABITS

Every morning when I get up
I know my day has just begun,
But, I realize, for other people
So many things, they've already done.

Some people get up real early
So they can take a hike,
And after their walk is over
Some even ride their bike.

I've never been a morning person
But, I enjoy life just the same,
Now, isn't it great that we're all different
Because, that's the name of the game.

It doesn't matter if you're an early riser
Or if you stay up late at night,
It's what you do in between
That makes it wrong or right.

GOD'S WAY

As I sit here at my computer
Not knowing what to do,
I know it's time to get busy again
And write more poems for you.

I really don't have a subject yet
And I haven't thought things out,
But, I do know, when you write a poem
You write what you know about.

Just what do people talk about
Whenever they get together?
Well, to be on the safe side
They can always start with the weather.

AH, yes, the weather
I really do not know,
Why we are having all this wind and rain
But very little snow.

Here we are, in the month of February
And I am making notes,
I know it hasn't been cold enough
To get our heavy winter coats.

I'm thinking about two months ahead
And I know God has the powers,
But I'm wondering if He will send snow then
Instead of April showers.

Well let me get back to my calendar again
For I'm feeling mighty strong,
About God and His universe
He never does anything wrong.

WHAT IS FAITH

I know we should have a lot of faith
When God is working His plan,
But oftentimes we go ahead ourselves
And do all WE can.

And many times what WE want
Isn't what God has in mind,
For WE often want something else
Than that of God's design.

I had a situation recently
That God put in my way,
And I knew the only way to solve it
Was to come to Him and PRAY.

I wasn't the only one to please
There were other precious ones involved,
So, with a lot of praying and crying
The whole situation was resolved.

I am very happy and content
With the way that things turned out,
And what God wanted for my life
Is what I want too, I have no doubt.

So, thank you Lord, for putting me in that situation
I've gotten so much closer to you too,
And my faith has really grown stronger
And that's all because of you.

I AM A BOOK

Some people are consumed with reading a book
And there are many kinds, you know,
It could tell about their life
Or, the many places that they go.

It could be a love story
Or, even a big mystery too,
And some comedians even tell
About the jokes that they can do.

Now, in my book, I'm the main character
And I must be very careful what I do and say,
For I don't know who could be watching me
And I could very easily, lead them astray.

But, that is not what God wants for me
He wants my life to shine far and wide,
And when He allows me to meet someone new
I get such a warm feeling inside.

The best book to read is the Bible
It has all those subjects in it too,
And they are all contained in that one book
That makes it convenient for you.

If I live the life that God wants me to
And I know my actions are on display,
I might just be the only Bible
That someone reads, today.

HE'S WATCHING OVER ME

My God, You've been so wonderful
To me again today,
And I can't help but praise you
As I fall on my knees, to pray.

You understand my problems
For you care so much for me,
Your grace is so sufficient
And your Love, most satisfactory.

You understand my situations
You're interested in my every care,
And God, I feel so close to you
As I talk to you now, in PRAYER.

You protected me as a small child
You watched as I was running free,
And MY GOD, what satisfaction it is to know
THAT YOU'RE STILL WATCHING OVER ME.

MY GOD YOU GAVE ME EVERYTHING

My God, you gave me everything, you created this great earth,
You made it so very beautiful, I can't begin to see its worth.

You started with a piece of land, then you hung the sky in space,
And after you had worked six days, everything just seemed to fall in place.

You made the sun for heat and light, and the trees to give us shade,
It takes an awfully lot of faith, to believe, all these things, YOU made.

But then we have the Bible, and it tells us, this is so,
But it's only after we study it, that we can really, really know.

The flowers so very beautiful, the moon a'hanging way up high,
The stars with all their twinkling, make me begin to wonder, WHY?

You made the sea and the fish to swim, and the wind to make the wave,
The rain to refresh the plants and grass, are some more things that you gave.

The birds and animals seem so content as they wonder to and fro,
But there's nothing that is more beautiful than the fresh new falling snow.

The thunder and the lightning seem to make us be afraid,
Then we just sit back and think, God, this you too have made.

You gave up your son JESUS to Die for all MY SIN,
And I'm so glad that I am saved and that I'm following HIM.

I'm so grateful for all you've done and I want to say THANK YOU too,
But after looking back on all these things, I'm glad you gave me YOU.

ENCOURAGEMENT

Have you ever been so depressed
That you didn't know what to do?
And you felt such a distance from God
And thought He forgot all about you?

Then, suddenly, you met someone
It could have been a stranger or a friend,
That God sent to talk to you
And it was someone, on whom you could depend.

He has many, many angels
Walking down here below,
And he uses each one of them
To help show us which way to go.

It could be to encourage us
Or maybe give us hope,
Or even to extend our get-well wishes
In a simple envelope.

Could you be one of those angels
Who God is wanting to use?
And with all the encouragement needed
Just how could you refuse?

I'm so thankful that when I'm in that situation
God sends an angel to me,
So, thank you God for loving me so much
And making me a part of your family tree.

DOTTY COME HOME

It was one fall day in nineteen sixty-three
I went to visit My Mother,
And we had such a wonderful chat
She knew there would not be another.

When I left, she was standing on the porch
Yes, standing there all alone,
She was waving and calling to me
DOTTY COME HOME.

That next Sunday morning, while at church
Mom was walking down the aisle,
She was waving GOODBYE to everyone
And giving them her LAST BIG SMILE.

That night, it was about seven o'clock
My sister gave me a call,
She wanted my husband and me to come over
Because our Mother had a bad fall.

Well, she was lying on the couch
And a voice that sounded like a moan,
Was rolling and rolling around in my head
She was pleading, "DOTTY COME HOME."

Some years later I asked The Lord to come into my heart
And I'll follow Him to the very end,
And each day that goes by, I realize
I've never had a better friend.

Now, MY MOM is up there in HEAVEN
Close to JESUS, there on the THRONE,
And MOM don't you worry 'cause one day
YOUR DOTTY'S COMING HOME.

A LITTLE ADVICE

It's such a beautiful day today
The sun is shining bright,
And we yearn for a better tomorrow
After we've had such a terrible night.

God trusts us with His babies
That He gave to us to raise,
But, He also knows we'll stumble
And fall short in many ways,

He knows that we're not perfect
He made us just that way,
But, we know we can depend on Him
Today and every day.

It's hard to be a parent
We want the best for them,
And with our LOVE and GUIDANCE
We can help them around the bend.

Our Heavenly Father is right there
Stretching out His hands,
He wants to lead us down that path
And He makes no demands.

So grab a-hold and trust in Him
That's the best thing that you can do,
Then, here's a little reminder
This friend is praying for you.

POST OFFICE JITTERS

As you know, I like to write poems
And every week, I write another one,
People have asked me where I get my material
For all the writing that I have done.

Well, I talk to my Heavenly Father a lot
He knows I need Him every day,
And it doesn't take very long until
He sends some good material my way.

Like this week, I was talking to a friend
And I'll give him a fictitious name,
Because, after he reads this poem
He'll need some place to put the blame.

Sammy sent a check in the mail
And it didn't get to its right destination,
And when Sammy found out about it
It caused him quite a bit of frustration.

He went to the post office
To put a trace on his letter,
He didn't get very much help there
And it didn't make him feel any better.

He said that he wasn't much of a Praying man
But he didn't have much hope,
So he asked GOD to help him find
THAT PRECIOUS ENVELOPE.

Finally, that check did arrive
At the place where it was supposed to go,
But, in the meantime, it caused confusion
And the mail was rather slow.

I think GOD allowed this to happen to Sammy
Because He wanted more contact with him each day,
And Sammy had to realize not much was getting done
BY DOING IT HIS WAY.

A SPECIAL OFFERING

I heard about this friendly church
Way out in the countryside,
The welcome mat was placed out front
And the door was always open wide.

They had this special transportation
A bus, for those who could not drive,
The driver, very professional and never late
When at church, they did arrive.

One Sunday the usher told the Pastor
That there were buttons in the offering plate,
The pastor ran out to the bus
And told the driver to wait.

He thought, children or no children
Church is no place to be playing a joke,
He did not realize at all
How angry he was as he spoke.

He asked who put those buttons
In the offering plate today,
A little girl with big green eyes and scared
Not knowing what to say.

She said, "I did PASTOR
I didn't have any money,
So MAMA gave me these buttons and said,
'You can give these, Honey.'

"MAMA thought someone could use them
As they make some clothes,
I was so happy to give SOMETHING
But it was a bad idea, I suppose."

The Pastor, realizing He had acted badly, said,
"JESUS IS VERY PROUD OF YOU,
I really just wanted to thank you
Thank your MAMA too."

The buttons kept coming in week after week
And that's just the way that it was,
The Pastor said the bank doesn't want them
BUT JESUS DOES.

THE LITTLE OLD COUNTRY CHURCH

I started going to this little country church
Every Sunday night,
And from the first time I stepped inside that door
Everything seemed just right.

Now, this is a very little church
And not many people go,
But, God says where two or more are together
I'm there too, you know.

Everyone has made me feel so welcome
And they've done so from the very start,
And each one has a special place
Right inside my heart.

In the beginning of the service
We sing, maybe five or six songs,
They are ALL the old hymns
And that's the way it belongs.

Just before the prayer time
Pastor asks if there's a Special need,
There are always requests
That's a Special time indeed.

One night a man requested prayer
Because he was going to have surgery,
Two weeks later he was back
To thank God for his recovery.

Then, there's another precious man
Who is living a limited life,
He has that dreaded disease of cancer
And could soon be leaving his friends and his wife.

And there's the offering where we give back
Just a portion, as we've been told to do,
And the man who takes the offering
Has some Special needs too.

The Pastor always has a powerful message
His wife plays the piano too,
Their daughter sings and plays the organ
And their love for God comes shining through.

As we continue to worship in this little country church
It's very plain to see,
We are receiving so many BLESSINGS
My special friend and me.

MY CHINA STORY

I was awakened from my sleep last night
In the middle of a dream,
I heard God talking to me
At least, that is what it did seem.

God said, "You need another subject
That you should write about,
For instance, I'm thinking China
And you'll do well, I have no doubt."

I said, "God, I know nothing about China
You know, I hated geography in school,
But, if You head me in that direction
That would be really cool."

He said, "I'm not talking about the country, China
There's another kind of China, you know,"
And after a great deal of conversation
I realized just where He wanted me to go.

You see, I had visited a good friend
In a Nursing Home that day,
And she was very depressed because
Some unexpected news had come her way.

She had to be moved to a different room
Because she needed some extra special care,
And I believe this was the third time
Since she made her residence there.

She showed me all her Precious CHINA
In her China Cabinet that she had there,
And she was so sad because she knew
She must leave it behind, there was no room to spare.

As we walked to the cafeteria, I tried to assure her
That Our Heavenly Father really does care,
That no matter what room she is in
GOD WILL ALWAYS BE RIGHT THERE.

THE LOST CARROT

I've written so very many poems
That I'm running out of things to write about,
So when something crosses my path
I'll write about it, no doubt.

I have this friend who was eating small carrots
And she dropped one on the floor,
She looked and looked and looked and looked
But that carrot just was no more.

Then her niece came to clean for her
She looked for that carrot too,
They finally gave up because
There was no more they could do.

Now, I compared that LOST CARROT
To the CARAT that Gems are measured by,
And thought just how many Gems are in God's word
That slips by You and I?

So as we look more into His word
And come to Him more often in Prayer,
We will find more of those Precious Gems
That He has waiting for us there.

THE LORD IN MY SHOES

OH LORD, if you were wearing my shoes
Just what would you do today?
Would you stay at home and do some work
Or get dressed up and go away?

You see Lord, if I stay home
The phone is sure to ring,
Then I might talk about someone
Or say some cruel thing.

On the other hand, if I go away
Someone I'm bound to meet,
If I only go grocery shopping
Or just go walking down the street.

For then my tongue could start a'waggin
And I would get the same result,
For as soon as we would start to gossip
I'd know exactly who's at fault.

But, you know LORD, as I think of you
One thing I can safely say,
If YOU were wearing MY shoes
Things just wouldn't be that way.

A FRIENDLY VISIT

I met this man the other day
I went to see him in a Nursing Home
And when I got to his doorway
I realized, he wasn't alone.

His sister and brother-in-law were there
Having a laugh or two,
And their eyes opened real wide
When I stepped into view.

As I said, I had never met this man
But, some of my poems he had read,
So rather than send him another one
I went to visit him instead.

Now, he had never seen me before
And didn't know I was such a hotty,
He took one look at me and said, "I know you,
YOU'RE THAT POEM LADY, DOTTY."

Now, just how did he know that
For I am someone he never knew,
But I came to the conclusion
GOD had HIS hand in that too.

MY CAR

Some time ago, we purchased a piece of machinery
It was shining just like a star,
I was so happy we got it because
IT was MY CAR.

It held up very well for us
We drove it very far,
We went from Maine to Florida
IN MY SHINY CAR.

But, like everything else, it's wearing out
And I can't drive it very far,
But, each time I say, "GET ME THERE SAFELY
IN MY FAITHFUL CAR."

My children want me to get another one
And when it no longer passes the bar,
I'll be happy to say, "YOU SERVED ME WELL
YOU WERE MY CAR."

HAPPY NEW YEAR

With the Christmas Season over
And everyone is finished spreading cheer,
It's time to make New Year's resolutions
For Surprise, it's a brand new year.

It's time to take the tree down
And put all the decorations away,
And when I think of that
I know it's NEW YEAR'S DAY.

It used to be on New Year's Eve
We would go with our friends out drinking,
And as I look back, I say to myself
DOTTY, JUST WHAT WERE YOU THINKING?

Now I like to stay at home
And instead of POPPING a cork,
I like to watch the ball come down
And all the festivities in NEW YORK.

So, have a Wonderful Year, my friends
That's what it's all about,
BUT, maybe you would like to top it off
And have some PORK and SAUERKRAUT.

WHAT IS A VALENTINE

A Valentine is a Special card
You send to someone you know,
You have Special feelings for them
And you just want to tell them so.

A Valentine expresses LOVE
And it comes right from the HEART,
When the feelings are not returned
It can tear your HEART apart.

Now, I'm sending you this Greeting
But, I'll only ask one time,
Since it is VALENTINE'S DAY
WILL YOU BE MY VALENTINE?

PLEASE HELP ME LORD

Oh Lord, I come to You today
With gratitude and praise,
To ask for strength and guidance
To serve You in many ways.

And when You walk with me and talk to me
I ask that I will hear,
For I know I can serve You better
When I know that You are near.

So take my hand and lead me Lord
To where You want me to go,
For I know you really love me
BECAUSE YOU TOLD ME SO.

JESUS' RESUME

NAME—Jesus Christ
BORN—Christmas Day
WHERE—Bethlehem
PARENTS—Mary and Joseph
ATTENDING PHYSICIAN—God
PHYSICIAN'S ATTENDANTS—Animals in the Stable

LATER IN LIFE

OCCUPATION—Carpenter, Teacher, Healer
EXPECTED WAGES—Only Acceptance and Love

RAGS TO RICHES

Jesus was born in a dirty stable, on a stack of hay,
He wasn't born like other babies are expected to be born today.

And when He was a young boy, I don't know what they did for play,
But, I don't think they had soccer, golf, football, or volleyball, like today.

Then when He was only thirty-three, He hung on that Cross and was Crucified,
And it was for all of OUR SINS that He Bled and finally DIED.

Now He is living up in Heaven, walking on those STREETS OF GOLD,
And this is MY story of RAGS TO RICHES, and how it did unfold.

JESUS' BIRTH AND DEATH

I believe my favorite miracle is that of Jesus' birth,
How He was born and grew up to walk on this filthy earth.

Although He did many unbelievable things, He made the Blind to see,
He healed the Leper, made the Lame to walk, and all of this was FREE.

HE had the Twelve Disciples that He was training to take His place,
And I can't even imagine how it was, to see Him face to face.

Then, at the Last Supper Jesus knew, that when His earthly life ends,
Although He wanted to do God's will, He would certainly miss His friends.

The day came when Jesus was tortured, He hung on the Cross for all to see,
The two thieves hung there beside Him, as Mary, His Mother, wept bitterly.

They laid Him in a tomb, it was a sad, sad day,
But, later, Mary had reason to rejoice for the Stone was rolled away.

He ascended into Heaven and is preparing for us a place,
So as we go on our earthly journey, let's not, just take up space.

Now Jesus died for ALL of us, BUT, this we don't deserve,
So as we daily do His work, we should be very happy to serve.

As EASTER comes but once a year, it gives us time to meditate,
On all that He has done for us, so come on, LET'S CELEBRATE.

MY CHRISTMAS GREETINGS

A very Special Greeting
FROM MY HOME is being sent,
Because this is what your friendship
To me has really meant.

A year of peace and contentment
A year of Christian Love,
But none of this could have come about
If it wasn't for God above.

It was that tiny BABE of Bethlehem
Born of a Virgin Birth,
Born that first CHRISTMAS MORNING
Raised right here on Earth.

So a VERY MERRY CHRISTMAS
And a Prosperous and healthy NEW YEAR too,
And this is what I'm wishing
For each one of you.

GETTING READY FOR CHRISTMAS

Here it is December again
The busiest time of the year,
When children sit on Santa's lap
To whisper in his ear.

They tell him that they've been good
But when he looks into their eyes,
He can tell if that's the truth
Or whether it's all lies.

I love to decorate my home
With lights and mistletoe,
And when the tree is all lit up
The room has quite a glow.

And when it comes to cookie time
Just make no mistake,
Because all your love goes into
Every cookie that you bake.

Then I think of all the gifts you buy
For each one you hold dear,
You know that with your Credit Card
You don't have to pay until NEXT YEAR.

It's beautiful on Christmas Eve
If we can only have some snow,
Than you can almost see Santa on His sleigh
And hear His HO HO HO.

Well Santa, I've been good this year
Not like some other years before,
But Santa, I don't have a chimney on my home, so
JUST LEAVE ALL MY PRESENTS AT MY FRONT DOOR.

THE 4th of JULY

YES, it's THE 4th OF JULY again
Independence Day,
Another time for us to celebrate
Each in our own way.

Some had picnics, some went boating
Some relaxed at home,
Some ate out at a restaurant
Some visited loved ones on the phone.

I didn't do a picnic
And boating is not my thing,
But, I did relax at home
Then go to a restaurant with my KIN.

Yes, I talked on the phone
To my family who were out of state,
I also talked to my late Husband
There behind Heaven's Gate.

Then it came that time I look forward to
Each and every year,
When I sit on my front lawn
With loved ones I hold dear.

We looked up in the sky and saw
Sparkling red, white, and blue,
With green, purple, and orange
Oh, what a perfect view.

Oh yes, it was a glorious day
Even with the humidity and heat,
And talking to my Heavenly Father at bedtime
Just made that day complete.

MAKING ADJUSTMENTS

It was a nice warm sunny day
Although I was a little sad,
For I was cutting back all my old flowers
After a blooming summer, they have had.

And it took me a little longer this year
Then what it would usually do,
And I'm not saying it's because I'm older
But, that excuse will do.

I hate to see the summer go
With all its warm sunny days,
When I could sit out on my porch
And give My Heavenly Father, praise.

Now, another thing we must remember
It's that time of year when,
We have to make another adjustment
And turn all our clocks [BACK AGAIN].

THANKSGIVING MEMORIES

I was awakened early this morning
In fact, it was a quarter to three,
And that was a little strange
Because, that just isn't me.

As I lay there, I started thinking
About things that happened in the past,
And when God takes your loved one from you
It's all those memories that last.

I thought about Thanksgiving coming up
In just a very few days,
And how I am so thankful
And blessed in so many ways.

God gave my husband and me five children to raise
And we never had a lot,
But, we were always thankful
And contented with everything we got.

I remember one Thanksgiving
When things were a little tough,
We really didn't have very much
But, God saw that we had enough.

We gathered around our Thanksgiving table
And after we gave thanks,
We dug into our Thanksgiving feast
Of the best baked beans and franks.

God has brought me through many rough times
But, there have been lots of great ones too,
So, at this time of year, I say a Special Thanks
It's the appropriate thing to do.

Now, I know why I was awakened so early
It was because of this poem I was to write,
So now, I'm going back to bed
It's a quarter to five—Goodnight.

WHAT THANKSGIVING MEANS TO ME

We have made it through another summer
And most of November also,
The leaves are still a'falling
But we're not quite ready for the snow.

We're getting close to the 4th Thursday of November
And that is Thanksgiving Day,
It's another day to celebrate
But, what is Thanksgiving anyway?

Well, it's time for family and friends to gather
Around a table, with food so good,
And everyone eats way too much
At least, more than they should.

Let's see, it's turkey with all the trimmings
And lots of gravy too,
Mashed potatoes, candied yams,
And of course, stuffing for you.

Then there's baked corn, green bean casserole
Cranberry sauce and pumpkin pie,
And some people like apple cider
They can't pass that by.

Now, when we are so full and about to pass out
And you know that's really a shame,
They want to turn on that T.V. set
To watch a big football game.

Now, there's something about Pilgrims and Indians
And it's because of them that we are here,
And when they got together
They spread the first Thanksgiving cheer.

But, to me, Thanksgiving means something else
Thanking God for all His blessings that I hold dear,
But, I suppose there's quite a few people
Who won't thank God again, until Thanksgiving—Next Year.

SPRING IS HERE

When I looked out my window
Just the other day,
What I saw was two rabbits
Putting on a great display.

They seemed to be having so much fun
Doing their little dance,
And I enjoyed that, but it annoys me
When they nibble at my plants.

Oh, I know they are a part
Of GOD'S great creation,
So when I shoo them away from my plants
I do it in desperation.

That made me think about another rabbit
That shows up this time each year,
He wears his shiny white coat
And brings children lots of cheer.

He also brings a basket
Filled with candy, gifts, and money,
Now you know who I'm talking about
Of course, it's The EASTER BUNNY.

He always has so much fun
With all the kids who he holds dear,
And they have loads of fun with him
They know they have nothing to fear.

But, there is just one thing that puzzles me
And maybe you might know,
When Easter is over, and until next year
JUST WHERE DOES THAT EASTER BUNNY GO?

HAPPY EASTER

When we get to MARCH and APRIL
And the snow is a passing thing,
Here comes the EASTER BUNNY
Announcing that it is SPRING.

Oh yes, we decorate EASTER eggs
And get lots of candy too,
And most people get new clothes
Because the old ones will never do.

Now, all these things are wonderful
But, wouldn't we be at a loss,
If we didn't remember JESUS
And how HE was tortured there on THE CROSS?

Can we even imagine us taking HIS place
And all the pain that HE went through?
Well, just think about it my friend
And a BLESSED EASTER TO YOU.

MARY AND JOSEPH

Mary and Joseph went on a trip
And it must have been a little scary,
For there was a precious child to be born
And she was a Virgin, that Mary.

Now, Joseph was weary and Mary forlorn
As they searched for a place to stay,
For there was just no room in the INN
So in a stable, they slept on the hay.

That night a precious child was born
And the Wisemen came from afar,
And shepherds followed bright lights in the sky
This was their Guiding Star.

Now how would we feel if we gave birth to a child
And in a pile of hay he was laid?
And even being around all those animals
I don't believe they were afraid.

This Precious Babe came to save the world
And from OUR SINS HE WANTS TO SEIZE US,
Oh yes, I didn't mention His name
But, then you know it—IT'S JESUS.

JESUS' BIRTH

When I think of JESUS
And how HE came to this earth,
It was very different because
HE was of a Virgin Birth.

I believe that Mary was confused
When she heard what she was to do,
And Joseph, I bet he was excited
To be a part of this plan too.

Now isn't it interesting when the BABE was born
There was no place for them in the INN?
So in a stable with the animals
They all gathered around HIM.

Can you imagine, in a pile of hay
Your newborn child would be laid?
But, even with the animals there
I don't believe they were afraid.

Now, Jesus was born in a humble setting
Not in a sterile hospital, like today,
HE didn't have a nice warm crib
But settled for a nest in the hay.

Now we have all heard this story
Told over and over again,
But it's so nice to be reminded
Just how it was, back then.

A SNOWY SUNDAY MORNING

When I got up this morning, it didn't take much research,
To realize, I wouldn't be going to Sunday School and Church.

You see, over the night, a lot of white flakes came falling down,
So, as I looked out my window, I was satisfied, just to stay in my nightgown.

So, I played some of my Church tapes, some from way, way back,
And it brought back some memories, BUT, something it did lack.

And, I know what it was, there was just NO FELLOWSHIP THERE,
As I sat all alone on my RECLINING CHAIR.

Now, I know people say that they can get Preachers on their T.V. screen,
But, that's no comparison to Church, if you know what I mean.

When you mingle with God's Family, with a hug or shaking hands,
You are participating in the act of one of God's commands.

He said to LOVE one another, as I have LOVED you,
And that is my commitment to each one of you.

I'm looking forward to next Sunday, But, only GOD will know,
If HE will BLESS us with sunshine, or SURPRISE US WITH MORE SNOW.